# FORTY DAYS LOST

## AS TOLD TO BEN EAST

## ILLUSTRATED & DESIGNED
## BY JACK DAHL

## EDITED
## BY JEROLYN NENTL
## AND DR. HOWARD SCHROEDER

Professor in Reading and Language Arts, Dept. of Elementary Education, Mankato State University

### Library of Congress Cataloging in Publication Data

East, Ben.
  Forty days lost
  (Survival)
  SUMMARY: Seven men en route by air from iron mines in northern Quebec make an emergency landing in wild bush country and attempt to keep themselves alive for 40 days.
  1. Survival (after airplane accidents, shipwrecks, etc.)--Juvenile literature. (1. Survival) I. Dahl, John I. II. Nentl, Jerolyn Ann. III. Schroeder, Howard. IV. Title. V. Series.
TL553.9.E27            971.4'1            79-5185
ISBN 0-89686-042-6 lib. bdg.
ISBN 0-89686-050-7 pbk.


International Standard Book Numbers:      Library of Congress
    0-89686-042-6 Library Bound               Catalog Number:
    0-89686-050-7 Paperback                      79-5185


Adapted from the original publication *Narrow Escapes* by **Outdoor Life,** Copyright 1960.

## CRESTWOOD HOUSE

**P.O. Box 3427
Hwy. 66 South
Mankato, MN 56001**

71175

## ABOUT THE AUTHOR...

Ben East has been an *Outdoor Life* staff editor since 1946. Born in southeastern Michigan in 1898, and a lifelong resident of that state, he sold his first story to *Outers Recreation* (later absorbed by *Outdoor Life*) in 1921. In 1926 he began a career as a professional writer, becoming outdoor editor of Booth Newspapers, a chain of dailies in eight major Michigan cities outside Detroit.

He left the newspaper job on January 1, 1946, to become Midwest field editor of Outdoor Life. In 1966 he was advanced to senior field editor, a post from which he retired at the end of 1970. Since then he has continued to write for the magazine as a contributing field editor.

Growing up as a farm boy, he began fishing and hunting as soon as he could handle a cane pole and a .22 rifle. He has devoted sixty years to outdoor sports, travel, adventure, wildlife photography, writing and lecturing. Ben has covered much of the back country of North America, from the eastern seaboard to the Aleutian Islands of Alaska, and from the Canadian arctic to the southern United States. He has written more than one thousand magazine articles and eight books. Today his by-line is one of the best known of any outdoor writer in the country. His outstanding achievement in wildlife photography was the making of the first color film ever taken of the Alaskan sea otter, in the summer of 1941.

In recent years much of his writing has dealt with major conservation problems confronting the nation. He has produced hard-hitting and effective articles on such environmentally destructive practices as strip mining, channelization, unethical use of aircraft to take trophy game, political interference in wildlife affairs, the indiscriminate use of pesticides and the damming of wild and scenic rivers and streams.

In 1973, he was signally honored when the Michigan Senate and House of Representatives adopted a concurrent resolution, the legislature's highest tribute, recognizing him for his distinguished contribution to the conservation of natural resources.

# A FOREWORD TO FORTY DAYS LOST

I have written many stories about men who suffered terrible ordeals in the outdoors. Some got lost and wandered for days through thick woods where there were no roads. Others wandered in rain, snow, and cold without food or a fire.

Some were attacked by wild animals, usually bears. One man was so badly hurt in his face that, as he said afterward, he no longer had a face. Another was scalped by an angry grizzly.

Some people were struck by poisonous snakes and crippled for life. One person lost a leg above the knee from a rattler bite.

But of all the ordeal stories I have written, there is none I put ahead of this one.

Here are seven men, not even speaking a common language, with hardly enough food for four days. They are lost in a huge tract of wilderness with countless lakes and rivers where no human could possibly get out on his own. Radio calls for help, sent out from their grounded aircraft, bring no answer.

They eat frozen berries and mushrooms that they know may kill them. They even cook and eat moss. Rain and snow fall day after day. The men are cold and starving, and winter is almost on them. They see searching aircraft and set off smoke signals, but there is no response. The country is so big and wild that a tiny column of smoke is not noticed from the air.

While growing weaker they wait for more than a month to be rescued, knowing that death cannot be far away. And while they wait, the biggest air search in the history of Canada combs the roadless wilderness, looking for them.

The story was told to me by Robert Mullin, the pilot who took charge after his plane ran out of gas and was forced to land. I had never heard a story like it.

Experienced outdoorsmen have told me that they cannot read the account of the suffering of these seven men without tears of pity coming to their eyes. That is a feeling I share.

**BEN EAST**

Seven men were lost in the wild bush country of northern Quebec. None of them was a survival expert. Yet they kept themselves alive for forty days. All that time, they waited and watched for someone to rescue them. They tried to help themselves, too, but could not.

There had been no hint of danger when their adventure began. These men were miners on an airplane flight coming from the Eskimo town of Fort Chimo on the Arctic rim. They were headed for Roberval, on Lake St. John, seven hundred miles to the south. It was to have been a routine flight. The pilot, Bob Mullin, had been hired to fly the men out of the iron-rich far north country before the fall freeze-up. It was late August, and the job seemed simple enough. Bob found a nineteen-year-old crewman named Dick Everitt. After checking out all needed equipment before the flight, Bob carefully looked over his single-engine pontoon plane. Everything was ready to go!

Bob and Dick landed at Fort Chimo in a snowstorm the night of August 24. They were greeted with bad news. The men would have to fly back to Roberval the next day. A drilling boss had developed a huge lump on the side of his face and needed a doctor. Bob and Dick agreed to leave at dawn. They also agreed to take a full load of men and gear along with them. The summer's work was done and there was a waiting list of workers

eager to get home from the Arctic.

Morning dawned crisp and clear. The men quickly ate breakfast and got ready to leave. After taking off, Bob headed the plane south. They were traveling about one hundred miles-an-hour. A vast wilderness lay below. There were lakes and rivers, mountains and tundra. Much of it was not mapped. Bob planned to stop midway at a deserted weather station on Lake Nichicun. A few drums of gas were stored there and, by that point in their flight, he would need to take on more fuel.

The flight went well, although Bob and Dick had to fight strong winds all the way. Shortly after noon, they flew over the sprawling watershed of the Fort George River. Bob knew it from his maps and began to look for Lake Nichicun. The plane flew on and the minutes turned to hours. He could not see anything that looked like the right lake. Four hours had passed before he admitted being lost. The high winds had blown the plane off course.

Bob knew he could not make it home on the fuel which was in the plane. He also knew there was no other gas between Fort Chimo and Rober-val. Rather than risk running out of fuel in flight, he began to look for a lake where he could land. It had to be big and quite free of islands and rocks. He soon spotted one that looked good. It even

had a small clearing on the far shore. As he got closer, he could see a tent. He could do no better, so he gently set the plane down on the water.

He taxied to the clearing, and the men climbed ashore. The "tent" they had glimpsed from the air was not a tent at all. It was a shack built of log walls and covered with a tarp. The walls were sagging and the tarp had rotted and started to fall apart. The men believed it had been at least a year since anyone had used the place, maybe longer. It had probably been built by Indian trappers.

The men were not worried about being lost. Once Bob had sent an SOS message on the plane's radio, they were sure help would soon come. They began to sort through their supplies. As a shelter for the night, they set up the tent from the plane. They made ready for an emergency, just to keep busy. None of the men thought they were in any real danger.

The seven found they were quite well equipped for a short stay. The tent from the plane was a wall type, nine feet square. They had a gun and some ammunition. There was a fishing rod and reel plus a few lures and a net, three axes and a small crosscut saw. Two boxes of emergency rations, a kit of pots, pans, and dishes were also in the plane. A few odds and ends completed the list. There were three smoke flares, two flares for night signaling, a role of fine copper wire, and a small first aid kit. The ration boxes held enough food for two men to last fourteen days. For seven men, the rations would last four days. It was mostly canned meats, fruit juices, and beans. There were some dried soups and vegetables, powdered milk, and chocolate bars. There were three packs of tobacco, too. However, there was no sugar, no fat for frying, and very little salt. There was less than a pound apiece of tea and coffee, and only a little flour. It was not much, but the men did not think they would be stranded for long.

While the men were checking supplies, Bob went to send a radio call for help. The air waves were full of traffic, but no one answered his call. He sent the message and listened for a reply several times. Still, no one answered. A small chill went up his spine. He was not getting through to anyone! Bob knew radio transmissions could be uncertain in the far north country. If no one heard him today, someone would surely hear him tomorrow.

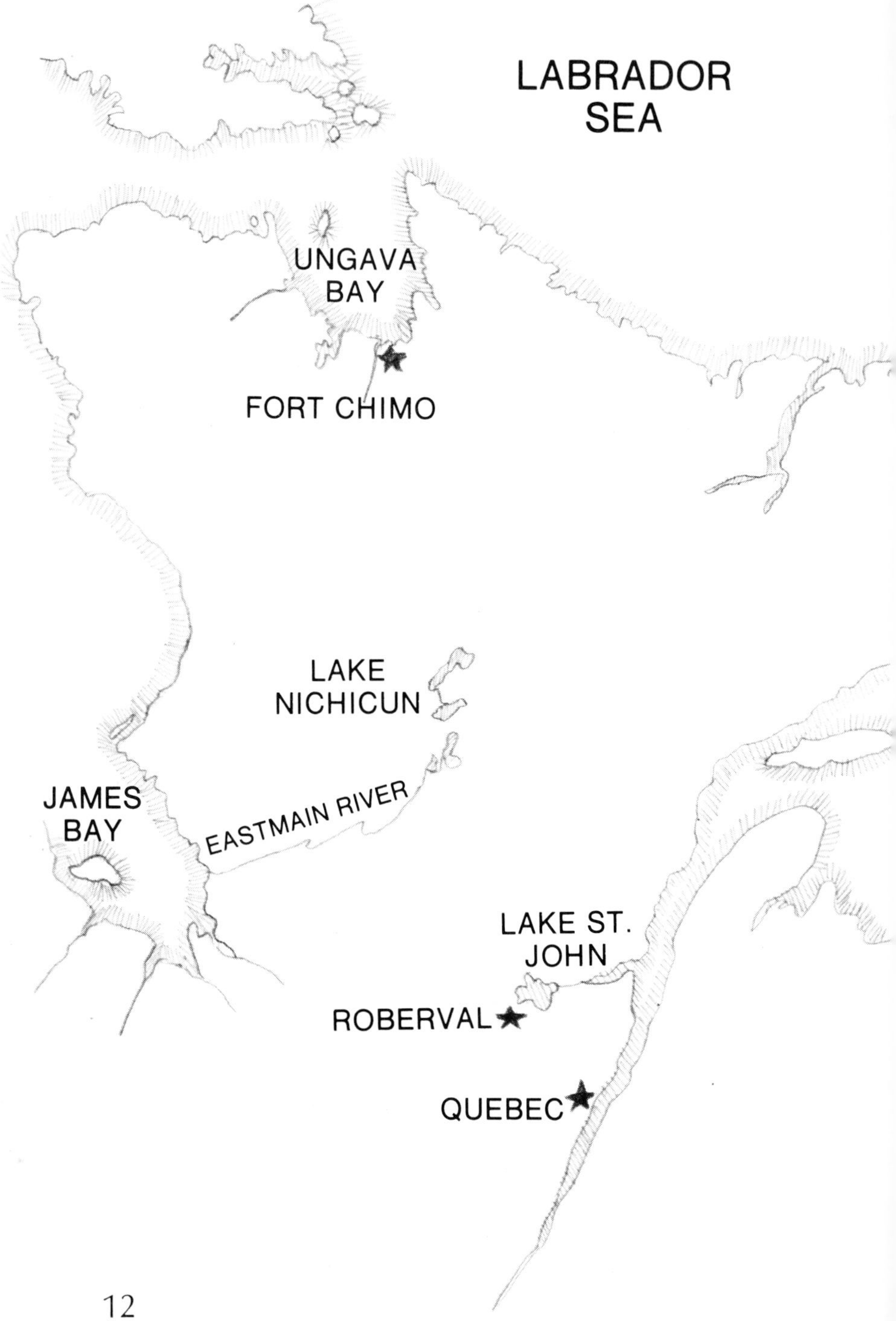

LABRADOR
SEA

UNGAVA
BAY

FORT CHIMO

LAKE
NICHICUN

JAMES
BAY

EASTMAIN RIVER

LAKE ST.
JOHN

ROBERVAL

QUEBEC

He joined the rest of the men and they opened enough rations to treat themselves to a light meal. They were all very hungry. The meal would give them a chance to get to know each other, too. They were strangers, brought together by accident. Bob had known Dick only a few days. The other men he had known since morning. The five which were picked up at Fort Chimo knew each other only slightly. Two of them were from Europe. Rolphe Theinhaus was a geologist from Germany and Klaas Koeten was a mining engineer from Holland. They had come to Canada to look over the iron mines at Fort Chimo. Victor Abel, the drilling boss who was sick, was from Quebec. Except for the pilot, Victor was the only experienced bush man in the group. However, he was too ill to be much help. Marc Levesque was Victor's helper and was also from Quebec. Ray Vanstone was a twenty-year-old student who had worked in the mining fields during the summer.

The lost men sat for a long time in their tent eating and talking. They knew they could not walk out of the vast wilderness. It was much too far. The country was too rough. There were too many rivers, lakes, and streams. They had landed in the great triangle of wilderness north of the St. Lawrence River and east of Hudson Bay. Lake Nichicun had to be somewhere nearby, but the men did not know which way to go. The nearest settled country was around Lake St. John, three hundred miles south. Fort Chimo was four hundred miles north. They could see no other way but wait to be rescued. There was a chance that the Indians, who had built the fishing camp, might return. But that was not likely. The canoe racks were

empty, and there was no equipment or supplies. It looked as if the place had been abandoned for good and no one would return. An official search was their best hope of rescue. The problem would be for searchers to find them in such a vast wilderness. No one would know their location if Bob's SOS calls did not get through.

The men agreed they had to do all they could to help the searchers spot them. They decided to move the plane out to the middle of the lake where it would be better seen from the air. First, they had to build a raft so they could ferry back and forth. They also agreed to gather wood and green branches. They would need them for a signal fire which would send up a smoke column if they heard any search planes. It would be best to build this on a hill. One man would stand watch from dawn to dusk, ready to light the fire if a search plane were heard. They decided a man would also stand watch by the fire in camp each night. He would keep a flare ready, in case a search plane flew near them.

The men went to sleep that first night feeling very good. They were quite certain their radio signals would be heard, and someone would fly in a fresh supply of gas. Once the plane was refueled they would be on their way.

Help did not come. No one came to rescue

them the next day, or the next. As long as they were able to power the radio, Bob sent his SOS call. Each time, he would hold the line open for ten seconds. He hoped it would give those listening time to get a fix on the location of the lost men.

No reply ever came. The signals went unanswered day after day. The men had to settle down to the grim work of surviving. They would have to live one day at a time, for as long as they could. They would have to live off the land, hunting and fishing and finding berries and roots for food. What rations were left from the plane they gave out a little at a time. They agreed to save most of them for a final stand against starvation.

Bob acted as leader of the group. He was a bush pilot, with six thousand flying hours behind him. Part of his flying time was from his years in the Canadian and British air forces during World War II. The rest of it was from bush flights over the remote land of Alaska and Canada. The bush was nothing new to Bob Mullin. He had seen a lot of it both from the air and the ground. This was the first time he had been forced down in it. However, he knew what a man had to do to stay alive. Bob made a vow. He would do all he could to get himself, his young crewman, and his five passengers home safely.

The endless hunt for food began on the second day. During the time the men were lost only two fish were caught in the lake. They had found a few dry fish heads on a shelf in the shelter that, at first had raised their hopes. Patiently, they had cast their line into the water several times. At last, the reel wore out. After catching the two fish there had not been so much as another nibble. The men decided the fish heads had been carried there from another lake. There was no big game, either. It had taken only a few days of hunting to convince them of that. They saw no moose, deer, or caribou. They did not even see any beaver. No wonder the Indians had abandoned the place! If help didn't come in a week or so the men would be hungry enough to boil and eat the shrunken fish heads!

The first week was not too bad. The men dipped sparingly into the small supply of rations. The

third day, Bob had the good luck of shooting a flock of five partridges. From that time the lost men hunted partridges daily, but the birds were scarce. In all, they killed about thirty. At night, the men made rabbit snares from copper wire. Marc and Dick checked the snares daily, but with little success. They caught only five, one of which they shot with the gun. They also shot two red squirrels, but that was not much meat for so many men.

"We're getting lighter," Ray and Dick told the group one day. They had just come back to the tent from a trip out to the plane on the raft.

"When we first built the raft, Dick and I couldn't ride it without getting our feet wet," Ray told them. "Now it floats the two of us high and dry!"

The fact that all of them were losing weight was not news. There was hardly any food.

The lost men took turns picking blueberries. There were lots of them at first, but the freezing weather quickly finished the crop. The men would come back to camp after a whole day of searching with no more than a cupful of berries. By the end of the second week, they would bring back any kind of berry they could find. Red or black or green, they cooked them all. They were tasteless, but helped fill the aching emptiness in each man's stomach.

"The mushrooms in the woods near camp look like those I have eaten in Europe," Rolphe said while sitting around the fire one night. "I'm going to try them. If they don't poison me, we can all eat them."

The rest of the men had seen the mushrooms, too. So far, no one had dared to eat them. Rolphe was the first to take the risk. He gathered his courage, and ate some. The men waited and watched to see if he would get sick.

Nothing happened. A day later, Rolphe was still as healthy as the rest of them. The group added mushrooms to their skimpy menu. From then on, the daily meal was berries and mushrooms boiled together. Many nights there was only a spoonful for each man, but no one grumbled.

The best days came when someone shot a partridge or snared a rabbit. The men would grind up the bones, head and all, and boil them with the meat. They would wash the insides and add them to the pot, too. If it was a partridge, even the beak and feet would be ground and eaten. The meat was divided equally, a spoonful at a time. The broth was never eaten at the same meal. It was saved for breakfast the next morning.

There was no time to spare by day. Every minute was used for searching for food, watching for rescue planes, and working at other camp tasks. Once the sun went down , there was not much to keep the lost men busy. Poor as they were, the meals became the highlight of each day. The men would sit and talk for hours about what needed to be done the next day or about being found. Victor was reading a book about a search for lost men that failed. For a time, the men talked a lot about it. Victor had been lost in the bush twice before. The first time, he had walked for two weeks before meeting a group of Indians who led him to safety. The second time, he had to kill half his sled dogs for food before he was found.

"But this is worse," he said firmly one night by the fire. Klaas agreed. He had spent almost four years in a prison camp during World War II. One night he confessed that he would rather be there than take what the seven of them were going through.

As the weeks dragged on, the men no longer talked of searches or being found. They talked about their homes and families.

"I was married seven years ago October 2," Klaas said one night. "I hope I'm home by then."

At night, the men worked crossword puzzles or read some of the books they had with them.

Ray made a deck of cards from cigarette cartons. There was nothing else to do from dusk to dawn except sleep, and sleep was not easy in the cold, wet weather. The men were out of tobacco, too. In its place, they smoked leaves, bark, and old coffee grounds.

"You know what I dreamed last night?" Ray asked the others one morning. "I dreamed about a harvest dinner, the kind we used to have on the farm. Chicken and potatoes and all the trimmings! Boy, oh boy!"

That day, Bob used the last of the flour and a scanty supply of frozen berries to make a "blueberry pie." There was no sugar and the berries were not all blueberries, but it did not matter. The "pie" helped lift their spirits.

　　As the weather got colder, both the
mushrooms and the berries were harder to find.
Bob knew they had to have something else to eat
or they would die of starvation. One day, while he
was on fire watch, he tried some caribou moss. He
had heard that it could be eaten, and there was
plenty of it on the hill behind the camp. There
were several kinds. Some were green, some black,
and some were gray. Bob tried the wrong kind

first, and was very sick for two days. When he felt better, he tried again. This time he tested the gray moss and did not get sick. Once the men learned how to cook it, it was all right. They would boil it and dry it in a pan until it was brittle. Then they made it into a fine powder. From then on, there were many meals made out of powdered moss.

The men were losing a great deal of weight. Their skin hung on them like wrinkled leather. Their cramps and pain, dizziness and nausea grew worse each day. Cutting firewood was to much for them. Walking was a fearful ordeal. Each task was now an agony. Camp chores were done in shorter and shorter shifts, and the men lay down to rest very often. One day, Victor walked to the edge of camp to cut a small tree. He struck a few feeble blows with the ax, and then it slipped from his hands and fell to the ground. "I can't do it," he groaned as he turned back to the fire. The others helped support him.

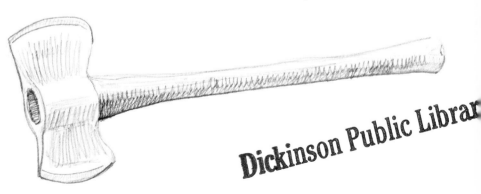

25

The weather stayed wet for days with a mixture of rain, sleet, and snow. The tent leaked and the sleepings bags were soaked night after night. At first, Bob and Ray paddled out to the plane and tried sleeping there. Twice they had to stay in the plane all day and through a second night without heat or food. The wind was so bad they could not make it back to shore.

Somehow, they had to get heat into the tent. Bob began making a small stove out of a ration box. He used empty food cans to make the door, the draft, and a short length of stovepipe. To his surprise, it worked. After that, they all slept in the tent with the stove, a small pile of dry wood, and the rations. It was crowded, but at least they were warm.

Things grew worse each day. None of the men had enough clothes. Ray had no windbreaker or cap, and his boots were falling apart. Klaas's boots were wearing out, too. Dick had one wool shirt and two pairs of light cotton pants, but no heavy coat. Rolphe had only a suit and a light cotton fishing outfit. Together the men had three parkas and a leather jacket, but no heavy underwear or enough gloves to go around.

The first search plane had been heard after seven days. It was flying behind a ridge off to the west. Bob was out on the raft fishing at the time, but the others set off a smoke bomb. It did no good. Two days later, they caught the hum of a plane again. It was early in the morning, and this time they saw it coming. It looked like it would pass within two or three miles of them. The sky was bright, with a few broken, fleecy clouds. The men waited until the plane was almost over camp and they touched off the second of their three smoke bombs. The instant the orange smoke poured out, a cloud cut off the pilot's view! When the plane came out from behind the cloud, it was too far south for the pilot to see the smoke. The men thought of that little white cloud as if it were a bitter enemy.

The lost men had no way of knowing about the search for them. At times there were as many

as forty aircraft looking for them. Pilots flew over more than 200,000 square miles of wilderness searching for any sign of the men. They looked for a thread of smoke from a campfire, a scar of broken timber, the wreckage of the plane. There was nothing. Volunteers sat next to their radios day and night. Now and then, they would pick up a garbled signal. Each time it was too weak to get a fix on the location of the downed plane. The signals only proved that at least some of the lost men were alive.

During the fourth week the plane ran out of gas. Without the plane's engine, Bob could not use the radio. It would be an accident if they were found now. Bob knew from his air force days that the searchers would look for them as long as there was hope. He also knew that sooner or later the search would have to be called off. In his mind, he set thirty days as the limit. The darkest hours of all came when those thirty days were up. He forced himself to accept the fact that they had been abandoned for dead. If they got out now, it would be on their own. There was only a slight chance of that.

It is hard for men who are lost to give up hope when they know that someone has been looking for them. It is hard, too, for searchers to give up hope and quit. It is very hard, indeed, if they know the people they are looking for are alive and waiting to be found.

To keep their minds off death, the men began stuffing moss into the cracks in the log walls of the old shelter. Their strength was almost gone, and they never finished the job. It was too much for them. Victor was very sick and the men had not been able to do anything for the sore on his face. They bathed it with warm soda water and gave him a few aspirin but that was all. He had constant headaches and suffered terribly.

The men tried to help themselves. Dick and Marc paddled across the lake and tried to set fire to the woods on the far shore shortly after they landed. They had hoped a fire would attract the attention of the searchers. When this failed, they tried to burn an island in the middle of the lake. That failed, too. Everything was too wet.

They went on one hike after another to try and find out where they were. If they could find which way to go, the strongest of them might be able to walk to Lake Nichicun. Then help could be sent back for the others before it was too late. The hikes were rugged trips. The men had to climb hills, walk across bogs, and wade waist deep through icy streams. They had to sleep without a bag, with no shelter except what they could make from tree branches. By the end of September, the lost men were desperate. If they could not find their way to Nichicun soon, all hope was gone.

The last hike was made by Rolphe and Ray. They trudged off one morning in a freezing rain, looking more like walking mummies than men. They returned on the second day drenched from the rain, cold, and exhausted. The men fell into their sleeping bags. It had been the worst trip of all, but they brought hope that lifted the spirits of all seven men.

From the top of a low mountain to the north, they had sighted a big lake. They were sure it was Nichicun. If they were right, their camp was on Lake Patamisk. It all matched what Bob saw on his maps. The outline of the lake looked the same. So was the lay of the land around it. All the other lakes they had sighted to the north on other trips seemed to match, too. It meant they were less then ten miles south of the lower end of Nichicun! Most of them could still walk that far. They could build another raft to cross the lake to the weather station.

The seven men agreed on a plan. They would split up and make a try for the weather station. Ray would stay with Klaas and Victor. His boots were about worn out, and the other two men were much to sick to travel. Bob, Rolphe, Marc and Dick would hike to the big lake. If they found it was not Lake Nichicun, they would try to return to camp.

Morning dawned bleak and cold, and snow was falling. Dick, Marc, and Ray decided to hunt first and went ahead in the direction of the lake. It was afternoon when Bob and Rolphe met up with them. The hunters had a warm fire going, and there was good news. They had shot a partridge! For seven starving men, it was not much food. It was badly needed back at camp. Yet it might mean success or failure to the four men trying to reach Lake Nichicun. The lives of all the lost men depended on the weather station. There really was no choice. The

four would take the bird with them on the trip.

It was a sad parting. The men shook hands, turned slowly and walked away. No one looked back. Neither group believed they would see each other alive again.

Having said good-by to four men, Ray turned around and headed back to camp to stay with the two sick men. The four others started out toward Lake Nichicun without another word. They walked steadily until dark, their spirits as gloomy as the day. They stopped for the night at the spot where Rolphe and Ray had camped on their last trip. Very tired, they started a fire and built a shelter of tree branches. That night, the partridge was cooked for dinner. The hot meal renewed a spark of life in each of them. They needed the extra strength they got from the meal, too. It snowed hard that night, and the wind blew even harder. The four men lay huddled among the tree branches, half frozen in their wet clothes. They were terribly discouraged and did not sleep much. It seemed as if morning would never come. Was this to be the end?

Day dawned at last. The four men warmed the broth from the partridge, and then continued northward once more. They stumbled through deep gullies, crawled up hills, waded streams and staggered across one swamp after another. Bob

had hoped they could make it to Lake Nichicun that day, but the hike seemed endless. Marc complained more and more often. He was getting very weak, and Bob feared he would not last the day.

Shortly after noon, they reached the hill from which Rolphe and Ray had first seen the lake they thought was Nichicun. It was big, and it looked right. No one knew for sure. They trudged toward the shore, but were forced to stop often to rest. About three o'clock the hum of an airplane engine broke the silence of the woods. The men strained their ears. It was coming from the north and the sound was getting louder and louder!

"My God, he's coming toward us!" Dick shouted. The plane was no more than two hundred feet above the trees and it was flying straight at them.

Bob fumbled in his pack for the flares. As the plane flew near, he fired one right in front of it. The flare streaked toward the sky, a faint spark in the daylight. The plane roared ahead as if nothing had happened. The men waited numbly while the hum of its engines died out in the south. No one said anything. None of them had ever known such heartbreak and despair. Less than fifteen minutes later, they heard it returning. Again it roared by, almost overhead. Again, they sent up a flare, and again it was not seen.

The lost men heard planes again toward dusk. They were to the south this time, but the men did not believe they were search planes. It had been forty days and they were sure any search had long ago been ended.

The search for them had been called off, as they had guessed. Then, at the urging of the lost men's families and friends, it had been resumed. When no more radio signals were heard, the search ended a second time. Toward the end of September, the unexpected happened. Canada's mine inspector visited Fort Chimo, and the miners urged him to try once more to find the lost men.

"We know they came down alive," the miners told him. "They're in there somewhere, on one of the lakes. The freeze-up will finish them."

The inspector agreed. He ordered search planes into the air once again. It was a last effort to find the lost men before they starved or froze to death.

The four men trudging toward Lake Nichicun had no way of knowing any of this. As darkness settled over the woods, they made camp once more. They opened and ate one of their small tins of beef. Without it, they could go no farther. They kept a fire going and lay under a flimsy shelter of tree branches. It snowed and the wind whipped at the little shelter. No one slept that night.

When dawn came, Bob and Rolphe set out to climb the last few hills that were between them and the shore. By eight o'clock, they had staggered up the crest of the last hill. They looked down on the lake, and then stared at each other. Neither man said a word. The lake before them was not nearly big enough or dotted with enough islands to be Nichicun. This was the end, for sure. The two trudged back to tell Dick and Marc the bitter truth.

There was no choice now but to try and make it back to camp. Could they do it? If they could somehow get strength into their bodies, they might be able to make it. They began to scrape together a meal of frozen berries and moss. The men were crawling around the snowy hillside on their hands and knees looking for food when the sound of a plane broke the silence again. This one was coming from the south. It was skimming the top of the trees. Their hearts almost stopped, and then the four men went wild! There on the open hillside, with their fire still burning from the night, they had a chance of being seen! Rolphe stumbled toward the fire to build up a smudge. Bob and Dick ran for the crest of the hill, slipping and staggering. Bob whipped off his shirt to wave as a signal. The plane roared over the brink of the hill, barely clearing the trees. The men waved as hard as they could. Even Marc made it to his feet. He stood there painfully waving his arms like a windmill!

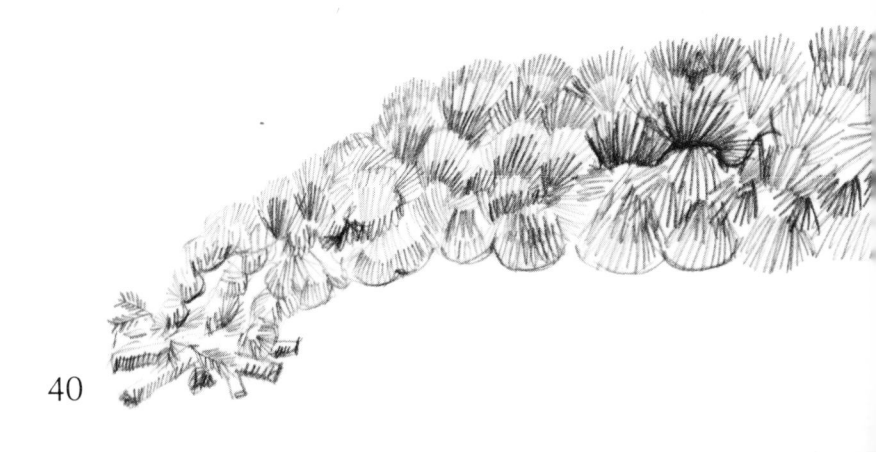

The huge plane lumbered off into the distance, and the men watched hoping they had been seen. Then it slowly dipped one wing, made a wide turn and headed back. It came straight at them. They had been found! The date was October 3. They had been lost for forty days.

"Stand by for a parachute drop!" a voice boomed from a loudspeaker in the belly of the plane. Soon an orange chute opened and floated down toward them.

"Stay by your fire," the voice boomed again. "We'll land on the lake and send in a walking party."

The men stumbled across the hillside to pick up the supplies that had been dropped. There was chocolate and biscuits, meat and salt as well as mittens, socks, and moccasins. The men ate the salt first. When all the food was gone, Bob started out to meet the walking party. They were within yelling distance before he saw them. He had not known until that moment that his eyes were failing him.

The lost man and the searchers met on an open hillside. It was as dramatic a scene as any moviemaker could produce, but no one could think of anything to say. All they did was shake hands.

"Hello," Bob mumbled. Then he asked for a cigarette. "What about the others? There are three more of us back at our camp."

"They were found yesterday afternoon. They're on their way out now," the searchers explained. The plane that had missed them had spotted the others. The pilot was not able to land on the water, but had called for help. Ray, Victor, and Klaas were alive and well.

The searchers carried Marc to the rescue plane, but the others could walk. The huge plane rose into the sky, and in minutes the whole adventure was behind them. They caught a last glimpse

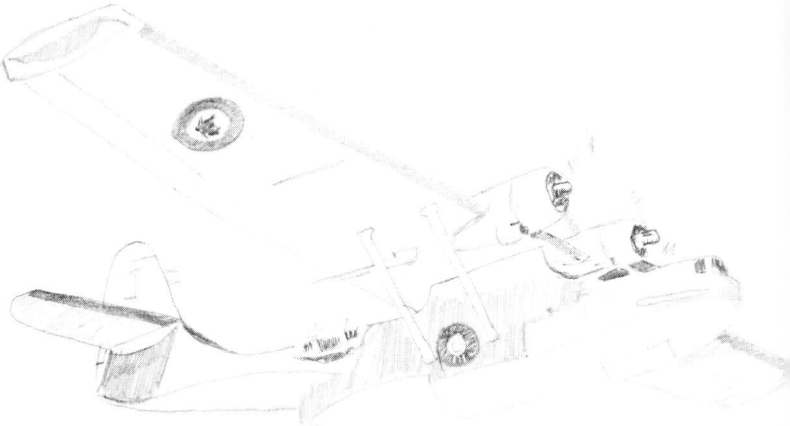

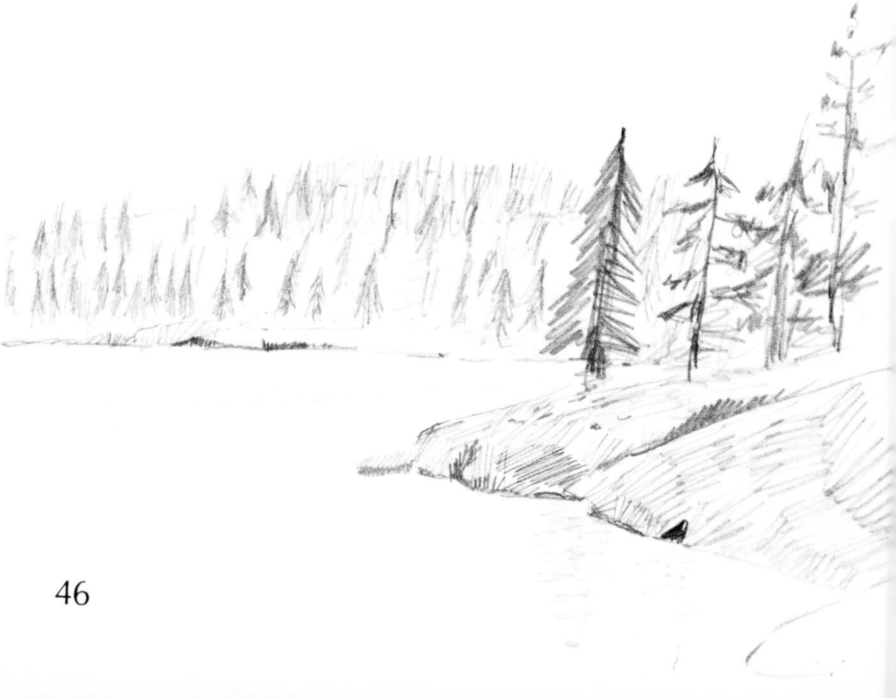

of their clearing as they flew toward Lake St. John. It was empty now and covered with new snow. There was no sign of life for miles around. Gas had been brought in, and their downed plane had been flown home. It was hard to believe they had spent those terrible weeks down there.

Marc was the only man needing an ambulance when they landed. Rolphe felt so good he did a little dance as he stepped out of the plane. Once at the hospital, Bob was surprised to learn he was as bad off as Marc. The two of them were ordered to bed, and put on a special diet. But they were lucky. They showed no lasting signs of the ordeal. Neither did any of the other men. It took only a few months to get them all back to their normal lives. Doctors told them that the moss had saved their lives. Without it, they would have starved to death. They learned, too, that they had landed on Lake Emmanuel, on the Eastmain River. They had been nowhere near Lake Nichicun!

They had been an odd crew to face such a challenge together. From the start, each of the men had put the welfare of the group ahead of his own. Their survival was a tribute to the respect and kindness with which they treated each other. It was also a tribute to man's will to live. The seven strangers survived an adventure few men would have lived to tell!

# Stay on the edge of your seat.

**Read:**

**FROZEN TERROR**

**DANGER IN THE AIR**

**MISTAKEN JOURNEY**

**TRAPPED IN DEVIL'S HOLE**

**DESPERATE SEARCH**

**FORTY DAYS LOST**

**FOUND ALIVE**

**GRIZZLY!**

**SURVIVAL**

**TRUE STORIES**